Lunch break with God

30 bite-size reflections to feed your spirit

Fr. J. Thomas Munley

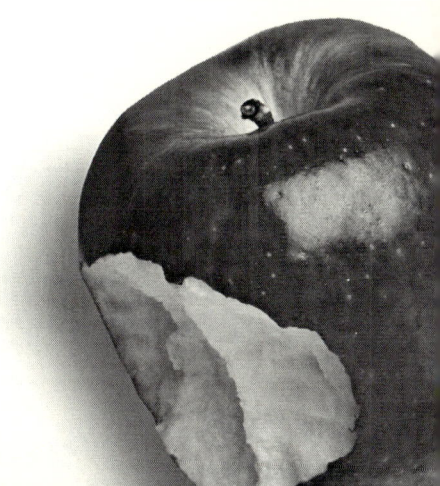

Copyright 2008 FAITH Publishing Service
All rights reserved. No part of this publication may be reproduced, stored in a retrieval system, or transmitted, in any form or by any means, electronic, mechanical, photocopying, recording, or otherwise, without the written prior permission of FAITH Publishing Service, 209 Seymour St., Lansing, MI 48933.

www.faithpublishingservice.com

International Standard Book Number (10): 0-9790747-2-x
International Standard Book Number (13): 978-0-9790747-2-1

Cover and text design by Lynne Ridenour
Faith Publishing Service

Artwork by www.istockphoto.com

Distributed by University of Chicago Press, 1427 E. 60th Street Chicago, IL 60637

Printed and bound in the United States of America.

My overwhelming gratitude to
my friends and family who have encouraged me to
write and believed that I had something to say.
A special thank you to my Patty Sue; you have been mother, sister,
guide, guru, sounding board and sometime secretary.

Christine & Ed,
Many Blessings and peace!

Menu

1	May I suggest
5	A loud silence
9	As long
13	Bridges
17	Beyond what is
21	Commitment
25	Conversion
29	Death becomes you
33	Expectations
37	Feed me
41	First light
45	Give me a break
49	God's breath
53	I don't understand
57	In between diapers
61	I putze, therefore, I am
65	Love, quiet, shhh, peace
69	My father was a gentleman
73	One child
77	Passion Sunday
81	Remember
85	Rose bud
89	The gifted curse
93	The many paths to peace
97	The secret
101	Today is the day
105	What are we praying for?
109	What if?
113	When Easter comes
117	Would we kill him again?

To the Reader

Thank you for purchasing this book. It is my hope and prayer that something in these pages will resonate with you and help you on your spiritual journey. The thoughts and ideas contained here have been born out of joy and pain. But they have been written with great fondness by remembering the lessons that are universal to all human beings: We are the loved and amazing creatures of a benevolent God. We are first and foremost loved. Everything else can flow from this beginning preposition. Unfortunately, the greatest teacher is always sorrow. I have come to realize that life is not fair or necessarily kind. However, it is in the living of this life that we grow, develop, mature and deepen our inner soul. Do not wait for life to become fair or pleasant or happy. Begin the work of self understanding and renewal where you are and who you are right now. That is what this book is about; understandings and new beginnings. Life waits for no one. Are you living the life you had hoped for? Are you the person you want to be? Begin now! Start with what you have in order to develop what and who you wish to be. No one is going to give you the time or the answers that you must carve out for yourself. Time is one of the most precious gifts you have. Do not waste one grain of sand in the hour glass. Knowledge is free! Self awareness is free! Spiritual depth and the gifts that flow from it are free! What a bargain. Why isn't there a line?

This book is not written as a novel. It is not meant to be read necessarily from cover to cover as fast as you can. It is meant to be read, prayed, thought-through, re-read, noted and marked in. It is a workbook for the Spiritual life. Bring your pencil. Plan to read one section at time. Each chapter is designed as one thought. Try to leave your judgments and pre-conceived notions of yourself, the world and religion on the doorstep as you enter the door of this book. The most profound lessons are normally contained in the simplest of truths. Bring your truth to mingle with these thoughts and see what God makes out of it all. Be open and you will always learn something. The moment we feel we have nothing else to learn is the moment we hasten toward our own early demise. Live, Love, Learn and Leave a Legacy.

Fr. J Munley

May I suggest

SCRIPTURE "Let love be sincere; hate what is evil, hold on to what is good; love one another with mutual affection; anticipate one another in showing honor. Do not grow slack in zeal, be fervent in spirit, serve the Lord. Rejoice in hope, endure in affliction, persevere in prayer." **Romans 12: 9-12**

REFLECTION

I am not a relationships expert. I have, however, become a marriage counselor by necessity. Between newly engaged couples and married couples on the rocks, I have heard and seen more than my share of crazy. I offer these five suggestions after years of listening and working with couples in various stages of maturity and healthiness.

5 SUGGESTIONS for a Happy Marriage

1. Date your spouse
2. Get on one knee: For forgiveness
3. Those who pray together, stay together.
4. Put as much time into your marriage each year as you put into the wedding plans the year before the marriage.
5. Love is not just a feeling: It is a covenant.

1 Date your spouse Growing up, every Friday night my parents went out to dinner. Almost without exception. My dad would take us 5 kids to Jack in the Box or Burger King and left my mother at home to get ready by herself. When we returned, a baby sitter would arrive and off they went. **That commitment to each other without kids and distractions helped them to communicate and foster their relationship.**

2 Get on one knee: For forgiveness I always ask newly engaged couples how the proposal took place. What happened, where, etc? Some of them are very creative and romantic. Almost every one of the grooms got on one knee to propose. That takes a great deal of humility. That is the basis for suggestion #2. **Each person in the relationship needs to muster enough humility to admit when they are wrong, ask for forgiveness and say those 3 powerful words; "I AM SORRY!"**

Fr. J Munley

3 **Those who pray together, stay together.** Prayer is one of those things we consider very intimate between us and God. **When you bring your spouse into this intimate relationship, you share with them the depth of the soul.** The two of you are bound with God in the most intimate embrace. It is personal disclosure at its deepest level.

4 **Put as much time into your marriage each year as you put into the wedding plans the year before the marriage.** If you look at the time, effort and money couples put into the year of preparation before their wedding day, it is sometimes staggering. If every couple put a fraction of that kind of effort and time into their marriage the first five years, there would be very little divorce. **Put the wedding in perspective and the marriage at the top of the priority list.** Mothers of the couple also need to take a chill pill. They are usually half the problem in overemphasizing fluff over substance.

5 **Love is not just a feeling: It is a covenant.** Love is not just a feeling. When the infatuation ends and the excitement wanes; what are you left with? Reality! **Love consists of knowing that you have made the commitment to someone else to stay and work, fight and pray for a healthy and loving relationship.** When all the sentiment dims, the true test of love is the ability to 'work out' and 'figure out' how to live and love another person even when running seems like the best option. Everyone changes over time. Everyone! Communicate, communicate!

Questions

What have you learned from past relationships that have soured that can be brought forward to inform how you enter and sustain new relationships?

Are you self aware enough to know what poor choices you make in relationships with others and can bad habits and unhealthy patterns be broken?

Do you repeat the same mistakes over and over with the people in your life? What do you feel it takes to sustain healthy relationships? Have

Personal notes:

A loud silence

SCRIPTURE "Then I saw in heaven another sign, great and awe-inspiring: seven angels with the seven last plagues, for through them God's fury is accomplished. Then I saw something like a sea of glass mingled with fire. On the sea of glass were standing those who had won the victory over the beast and its image, and the number that signified its name. They were holding God's harps, and they sand the song of Moses, the servant of God, and the song of the Lamb. "Great and wonderful are your works, Lord God almighty. Just and true are your ways, O King of the nations." After this I had another vision. The temple that is the heavenly tent of testimony, opened, and the seven angels with the seven plagues came out of the temple. They were dressed in clean white linen, with a gold sash around their chests. One of the four living creatures gave the seven angels seven gold bowls filled the fury of god, who lives forever and ever. Then the temple became so filled with the smoke from God's glory and might that no one could enter it until the seven plagues of the seven angels had been accomplished. " **Rev. 15: 1-8 (Modified)**

REFLECTION

> I sat,
> Quiet. Just sat
> And the snow fell and it was silent.
> Except the tiny sound of snow flakes
> Landing, everywhere, gently, yet; perceptively
> For snowflakes make a noise when they land.
> Small voices, crying, in the calm blanket of white
> because the world has been scarred
>
> The world has been scarred and silently,
> In the snow, landing, calling, begging
> The words came to me
> Asking if it must be this way
> And why? And what happened?
>
> I just want to stay here in the silence
> Savoring the gift of white, muffled calm
> Is that so wrong? To want to stay?

Fr, J Munley

But I worry and wonder:
What if this is it? The big one. Would they push it?
We seem to teeter on the brink.
There would be no turning back.

The world will change if that comes.
It will change for everyone, for the worse
We cannot go back. Once we have pushed it.

And so I sat, thinking, is this hush of muffled white
Is this it? This moment of silence and snow flakes.
Is peace only possible in moments, breaths and stolen pauses?
For now, I realize, this is all there is.
The world is crying, gasping, waiting.

And all of us know, we must learn to live with one another
as brother and sister
Or we will perish together as fools.
Before there was religion, and countries, and nations,
there was just 'us' and 'God'.
Before we divided ourselves into 'us' and 'them', there was just 'us'.
God's family. God's people. The Human Family.

Why must it be this way? Why?
Will it ever be any different?

QUESTIONS

Do you ever fear what may come to pass if we do not find inroads to mutual respect and survival of the nations of the earth?

Have you ever taken a stand or committed yourself to learn the issues at stake in global economics and political diplomacy?

ACTION PLAN

Learn one thing about another culture, religion or nation. We are becoming a global village. Know how issues around the world will affect you and our country.

Personal notes:

As long

As long

SCRIPTURE "You have heard it said, 'Love your neighbor and hate your enemy.' But I say to you, love your enemies, and pray for those who persecute you, that you may be children of your heavenly Father, for he makes his sun rise on the bad and the good, and causes rain to fall on the just and the unjust. For if you love those who love you, what recompense will you have: Do not the tax collectors and sinner do the same?" **Mt 5: 43-48**

REFLECTION

> As long as there are humans;
> There will be hatred and violence
> As long as there is hatred and violence;
> There will be bloodshed
> Where there is bloodshed;
> Innocent people will die
>
> When innocent people are killed;
> We are the least human of all

QUESTIONS

How consumed do you become with hating and wishing ill on those that have in any way hurt you? Do you ever get consumed by hatred of another?

Do you look into your heart and see love of others and their welfare or are you obsessed with getting even with those that have hurt you?

As a Christian, what is the difference between the way you are living and the way everyone else is?

Would anyone know you were a follower of Christ if they looked at your words and actions?

Do you like to see others succeed or are you always jealous and resentful?

What do the answers to these questions tell you about yourself?

Personal notes:

Bridges

Bridges

SCRIPTURE "Remember, there was a time when you were alienated from the community and strangers to the covenant of promise, without hope and without God. But now you who were once far off have become near by the blood of Christ. For He is our peace, he who made both one and broke down the dividing wall of enmity. Through Him we all have access to the Spirit." **Ephesians 2: 11-18**

(Pause and write down in the notes section of this chapter, what the scripture means to you. Then, read the reflection. Look at your notes again.)

REFLECTION

I love bridges. All kinds of bridges. From the huge expansion type that go across great spans of water to 'the small, homemade 2x4 type' that go across the creek in the back yard. Bridges have the capacity to join what was once divided. They bring separate things together that formerly where not. They merge opposites. They forge possibilities and unions.

We need more bridges; **People** who can bring other people together, even when they seem so far apart. We need people who can bring diverse and different people to one table and find a way to co-exist; Even if it is only for a brief moment in time. At least we would know it is possible. When will we find our way back to one another as a human race, a common people, a global community? Where does it start? Who **can** do that? Who **will** do that?

QUESTIONS

Who do you know that has been a 'bridge' in forging new relationships and bringing diverse people together for a common cause?

Are you a bridge builder or do you have a tendency to divide, to gossip and pass along rumors that hurt people and their reputations?

What qualities do we need in our leaders (government, business and religious) of today to bring about more common ground and create better understanding among people?

Personal notes:

Beyond what is

SCRIPTURE "There is a certain wisdom we express among the spiritually mature. It is not a wisdom of this age, however, nor of the rulers of this age, who are men headed for destruction. No, what we utter is God's wisdom: a mysterious, a hidden wisdom. God planned it before all ages for our glory. None of the rulers of this age knew the mystery; if they had known it, they would never have crucified the Lord of glory. Of this wisdom it is written: "Eye has not seen, ear has not heard, nor has it so much as dawned on man what God has prepared for those who love him." **1 Corinthians 2: 6-10**

REFLECTION

> The real challenge to the spiritual life is to see under what is evident; to look beyond to find the deeper meaning. It is to begin to see everything in life as sacred. It is beginning to see the meaning under the meaning. To know there is more. We often live life simply on the surface both in what we see and in our interactions with others. We greet people with, "How are you?", when we really don't want to hear the answer. We have the uncanny ability to keep people in the prison of their past mistakes never allowing them to show us what life has done in them since our last encounter with them.

> To live beyond the seen world to the unseen takes an awakening of spirit. It is the spirit of Jesus, risen and alive. As this spirit deepens within us, our awareness deepens along with it. Faith of any ilk or creed is a calling, begging, pleading to move beyond stale conclusions to fresh eyes. It is really about seeing. We can become very comfortable and thus complacent in our views and assumptions.

> This spirit is a longing, a soul journey that never quit gets satisfied here in this life completely. It is our quest as human and spiritual beings to reach beyond ourselves to the divine.

QUESTIONS

Do you ever feel as though you are simply skimming the surface of life without really getting to the marrow of what is most important or precious?

How does your faith and relationship with God inform your life, your choices, your relationships, if at all?

What assumptions have you made about life in the past that have enlightened you through living and prayer? Who or what helps you through the disillusionments we all encounter in life?

Personal notes:

Commitment

SCRIPTURE "What will separate us from the love of Christ? Will anguish, or distress, or persecution, or famine, or nakedness, or peril, or the sword? No, in all these things we conquer overwhelmingly through him who loved us. For I am convinced that neither death, nor life, nor angels, nor principalities, nor present things nor future things, nor height, nor depth, nor any other creature will be able to separate us from the love of God in Christ Jesus our Lord."
Romans 8: 35-39 (Modified)

REFLECTION

"The sad truth is that most evil is done by people who never make up their mind to be good or evil. " **Hannah Arendt**

- To commit is to take a stand
- If we are going to commit to something like religion and most especially to Christ, we are going to be controversial. Can you stand in the fire and proclaim your beliefs without flinching?
- In accepting the Nobel Peace Prize in 1986, Holocaust survivor Elie Wiesel said, "We must take sides. Neutrality helps the oppressor, never the victim." Silence, then, is a vote for those who oppress and not for the voiceless or the victim.
- We live in a throw away society. From meals to wheels to relationships, we want to move on to the next best thing.
- When it comes to Jesus Christ, we must be convinced that we have found the best thing. "The pearl of great price".
- Faith and religion (not always the same) are not just private matters, but also call us to examine the state of the community, town, country and world we live in.
- Commitment calls us beyond 'feel good' religion. Jesus is not an aspirin tablet, simply existing to help us feel good. There is always challenge in the Gospel message.
- In faith, we commit daily and must re-up just as in marriage, as in ordination, and like anything worth living for.

QUESTIONS

How trustworthy do you consider yourself?

When you make a commitment, do you follow through with it or do you have a tendency to 'drop the ball'?

Would others think of you as a committed person?

What would you say you are totally committed to?

What commitments do you regret not following through with?

ACTION PLAN

Write down one commitment you regret not keeping. Now, can you make it right? How?

Personal notes:

Conversion

SCRIPTURE "I declare and testify in the Lord that you must no longer live as the Gentiles do, in the futility of their minds; darkened in understanding, alienated from the life of God because of their ignorance, because of their hardness of heart, they have become callous and have handed themselves over to every kind of excess. That is not how you were educated in Christ Jesus, that you should put away the old self of your former way of life, corrupted through deceitful desires and minds, and put on the new self, created in God's way in holiness of truth." **Ephesians 4: 17-24 (Modified)**

REFLECTION

"The question to ask is not whether you are a success or a failure, but whether you are a learner or a nonlearner." **Benjamin Barber**

- Conversion is a type of learning. It is a learning of the heart with the eyes of faith. Conversion, like learning should be a lifelong pursuit. So often, people feel that as soon as their schooling years have ended, so has learning. This is often true of Christian people and the life of the Church. Once confirmation has taken place, young people are outa here. However, we are never done.
- The more I know, the more I know I don't know.
- Conversion can never happen without our cooperation and desire.
- Love is the greatest factor in conversion. Jesus loved people into new lives. He took them *where they were and for who they were* and then called them to a deeper, greater sense of self.
- Rules, laws and Doctrines are needed and necessary for us as an institution but they are normally not 'calls to conversion'. There are groups and individuals in Christian circles who want to beat people into conformity and belief. Faith must become a personal accent, a surrender of the self to Christ. You cannot force people into conversion
- The personal witness of others is one of the greatest calls to conversion and the reason why others want to know about Jesus Christ. Gandhi at one point was seriously thinking of become a Christian, that is until he met a number of them.

- They didn't live as they professed.
- Conversion can happen for many reasons, all of them valid, but normally fleeting. Conversion can result from the hard knocks of life, death of a loved one, personal loss, addiction, worship experiences, kindness of someone at a time most needed. This is where commitment normally makes an entrance.
- Both Conversion and commitment must be more than a feeling. Faith too is more than a feeling. It is like love. Marriage, ordination, family... to really be what they need to be, we must choose them daily. Feelings will only take us so far.
- Japanese proverb: *"Fall seven times, get up eight."* Conversion happens when we decide to get up again.
- Joan Puls in her book 'Seek Treasures in Small Fields' writes: *"We have the potential for rebirth and transformation, as long as we remain vulnerable to new experiences, to all we have yet to learn."*
- We will never experience conversion if we think we already have it all figured out. This stance lacks the openness needed for true conversion.

QUESTIONS

Have you ever felt so loved by God or another person that you wanted to make some changes in your life for the better?

Have you ever had a small or enormous conversion moment? What inspired it? How did you react?

What is another word for 'conversion'? Is conversion only a religious experience or can it be more? Other?

Personal notes:

Death becomes you

SCRIPTURE "Do not let your hearts be troubled. You have faith in God; have faith also in me. In my Father's house there are many dwelling places. If there were not, would I have told you that I am going to prepare a place for you? And if I go and prepare a place for you, I will come back again and take you with me, so that where I am you also may be. Where I am going you know the way. Thomas said to him, "Master, we do not know the way?" Jesus said to him, "I am the way, the truth and life. No one comes to the Father except through me." **John 14:1-6**

REFLECTION

One of my friends just passed away. I presided at his funeral the Monday of Holy Week. It was 2 days after his 54 Birthday. He died too young, too soon. Tim lived for 2 years past his original diagnosis.

While in the last stages of dying, Tim became more or less incommunicative. For the last two weeks of his life, he barely spoke; Very few words. He would react to a few things. But mostly he would lay silent.

As Tim was dying I began to wonder what he was *feeling*, what it was like for him. What was he *thinking* as he lay there. Was he in need of anything? Was he bored and just wanted it over? Was he sick of being sick? It was the first time I saw myself in a dying person. I don't mean I was just trying to relate to him. I was trying to crawl inside and look out. Not just looking on from the side of his bed. It was eerie and traumatic wondering what it must be like. The scariest realization was that there had to be a moment we will all face when we will all have to let go and jump into the arms of God. It is probably only a millisecond, but there was the awareness that we must let go of our spirit, our lives, our loved ones in this life to embrace the next.

That limbo, that small moment of blackness between this life and new life; when we shut our eyes and breathe our last; that is what haunts me; what if....?

Fr. J Munley

QUESTIONS

Have you spent time contemplating eternity? What comes to mind?

What do you think Heaven would be like? What about Hell? Do you ever fear going to hell?

Does the prospect of eternity in hell persuade you from any present behavior or make you remorseful for past sin or harm?

What do you think might tip the scale for you at the last judgment toward heaven or hell?

Personal notes:

Expectations

Expectations

SCRIPTURE Jesus said, "Then to what shall I compare the people of this generation? What are they like? They are like children who sit in the marketplace and call to one another, 'We played the flute for you, but you did not dance. We sang a dirge, but you did not weep.' For John the Baptist came neither eating nor drinking wine, and you said, 'He is possessed by a demon.' The Son of Man came eating and drinking and you said, 'Look, he is a glutton and drunkard, a friends of tax collectors and sinners.' But wisdom is vindicated by all her children. **Luke: 7: 31-35**

REFLECTION

> I tend to feel guilty. It is a dull, nagging kind of guilt. Not everyday or every moment, but enough. My guilt is really more a phantom than it is reality. It comes from the set of rules that I, "someone" else or "something" else has set up as 'the rule book of life'. I must try to live within the invisible 'wall of rules and regulations' or face the peril of attempting to leave the prescribed boundaries set up for me. I live with that dull guilty feeling that I have done something or have not done something that I or someone else has assumed I should do. I can get my head reeling with the thoughts of not being who I thought I would be; not being who they think I should be; not wanting to be who I am or wanting to be who I am without the mask of social approval. It is easy to get lost in the labyrinth of convention and behavior that come with each life situation and personal set of circumstances.
>
> As a priest, I realized early on that people want their ministers to be above the fray, without sin, perfect in word and deed. People don't want us to be vulnerable, get angry, feel pain, get tired, make mistakes, take sides or have favorites. At the same time they want to chum around, call us buddies, entertain and beguile them all while never really wanting us to be people at all.
>
> Expectations are hell. Expectations are the assumptions and presumptions we bring to every situation. They have the potential to do great things but also to cause a great deal of

harm or unrest. We bring our expectations with us everywhere we go and to everyone we meet. They are the shadow self. They become the voice that lives within us like some ghost that whispers continually in the mind. Expectations live in the cracks and crevices of the brain

Before we can harness the beast of expectation, we must know from where it comes. To name the beast is to garner power over it. From the very day of our birth, we are bridled with the hopes and dreams of our parents and grandparents. We come to silently internalize these hopes and dreams. We pick up more and more of these expectations as we travel through life, both from our own perspective and that of countless others. We make decisions based on what we have assumed we are supposed to do and be, only to wake up one morning realizing we have become a stranger to our deepest selves. Expectations have the potential to call us to higher ground but they also possess the ability to crush us with their weight.

Expectations that are clear and spoken are fertile ground for improvement and striving. But it is the unspoken or unrealistic expectations that are the breeding ground for disappointment and disillusionment. There is often a chasm between 'what is' and our perceived imagining of 'what should be'. It is in this divide that we begin to disappoint ourselves and others. What is it that can bring these two elements of life together?

My standards and expectations for myself are most often beyond what others would expect. This simple fact alone could be the recipe for disaster if expectations are not put into perspective and called into check through personal self knowledge. There is a point in life where dreams and lofty ambitions must mingle with stark realism and harsh facts. Somewhere between these two poles is a place called sanity.

Questions

Do you find yourself disappointed often? Why do you think that is? What lives behind that disappointment?

Do you think you have realistic expectations of yourself and others?

Where do expectations come from?

What are some of the unspoken expectations you assume as a spouse, Christian, brother or sister, friend or parent? How do these silently weigh on you?

PERSONAL NOTES:

Feed me

Lunch break with God, Vol. 1

Feed me

SCRIPTURE "Jesus withdrew to a disserted place. When the crowds heard of this, they followed him on foot from various towns and villages. When he saw the vast crowds, his heart was moved with pity for them, and he cured their sick. The disciples approached Jesus and said, "This is a deserted place and it is late, dismiss the crowds so that they may go to the villages and buy themselves food. Jesus said, 'There is no need to send them away, give them food yourselves.' But they said to him, 'Five loaves and two fish are all we have'. 'Bring them here to me', he said. Then taking the five loaves and two fish, he looked up to heaven, said the blessing, broke the loaves and gave them to the disciples who in turn gave them to the crowds. All ate and were filled. They numbered five thousand men, not counting women and children."
Mt. 14: 13-21

REFLECTION

> Do you ever just feel weary?
> Not of anything in particular.
> Just everything in general.
>
> Do you ever feel like you're starving in the midst of plenty? Like you're dying of thirst and drowning at the same time?
>
> These are the times that I think God is most tugging at our soul. Trying to get us to pay attention:
> To the right stuff; the good stuff; like health and friends and love and family and 'peace of mind' and 'peace of heart' and forgiveness and spirit.
>
> These are a few of the rare things in life that multiply without depleting anything else.
> These are the things that are self generating.
> These are the loaves and fish of today.
> These are the things we are starving for.
>
> But in this world of total abundance,
> Do we even know we are hungry?

Fr. J Munley

Spiritually hungry; emotionally spent, psychologically drained? We are hungry people gobbling up everything in our path.

What will it take to make us realize we are full? When have we have had enough?

QUESTIONS

Do you ever feel satisfied that you have enough? Enough food, sleep, material possessions, self esteem, love?

What are you hungry for? Is it always material things? Do you envy others and their possessions?

Can you ever be satisfied with what you have?

If not, what will help you to relieve the "hunger"?

Personal notes:

First light

First light

SCRIPTURE "When Jesus was born in Bethlehem of Judea, in the days of King Herod, behold, magi from the east arrived in Jerusalem, saying, 'Where is the new born King of the Jews? We saw his star at its rising and have come to do him homage.' After their audience with Herod, behold, they saw the star that had preceded them. They followed the star until it came and stopped over the place where the child lay. They were overjoyed and on entering the house they saw the child with his mother, Mary. They prostrated themselves and did him homage. They opened their treasures and offered him gifts. After being warned in a dream, they departed for their own country by a different route." **Mt 2: 1-12**

REFLECTION

It is really the darkness that becomes the birthplace of light. In the Scriptures, the wise men travel by night. The Magi are traveled in darkness, tricked by evil, but set upon a new path by the light they find in the innocence and the powerlessness of the Christ child. Our whole universe was born from darkness into light. The history of the world was changed by one birth.

God came to us without merit, money or power so that we may one day understand; all that holds value is not simply what we can wrap our hands around but wrap our hearts around.

It is in the darkness of our own journey that we must find the light. We are all sojourners; travelers in this life of unknown perils and possibilities. The light does not abolish all darkness; it simply leads the way as we travel through it.

In the darkness we still find a light that leads to the God of new beginnings and simple truths. The darkness is a dreaded but powerful teacher. In the silent blackness, we may find our greatest strength and most illuminating path.

We must not be too quick to throw off the darkness for in it may lie the beginnings of first light. When we sit with our own sinfulness, wounded soul and tortured spirit; it is then that

Fr. J Munley

we may find our way to new life because we have come to understand what we must leave behind.

The darkness teaches; the light leads.

QUESTIONS

What have your dark moments or difficult events taught you about yourself and others?

Do you have the courage to look deep into your own personal demons to find a path to light and freedom?

What keeps you from the light?

How does Jesus Christ and a loving God speak to the darkness you may find in or around you? What light does God bring to you?

To who or what do you turn in times of testing? Have you ever been so despondent that you thought about suicide? What kept you clinging to life?

Personal notes:

Give me a break

Give me a break

SCRIPTURE "Happy is the one who God reproves! The Almighty's chastening do not reject. For he wounds, but he binds up; he smites, but his hands give healing. Out of six troubles he will deliver you, and at the seventh no evil shall touch you. In famine he will deliver you from death, and in war from the threat of the sword; from the scourge of the tongue you shall be hidden, and shall not fear approaching ruin. At destruction and want you shall laugh; the beasts of the earth you need not dread." **Job 5: 17-22**

REFLECTION

What have I done to deserve this? How many times have we asked ourselves that simple question? It is the oldest question in human history other than *"where is the bathroom?"*

Sometimes daily we may find ourselves wondering what it was that we did to bring on the latest pain or inconvenience. At times the larger burdens of life feel like they may crush us. We turn to God and wonder why we are being punished. We search our minds and probe our hearts to try to figure out what we might have done; what divine law we may have broken; what offense have we given to God and are now paying for?

"I knew I should not have cheated on that test, stolen that stapler from work, gossiped about that girl I really don't know, looked at that pornography, or had that last drink."

The reality is there are always consequences for our actions. But the question remains, are they **Divine** consequences? Is God making a list and filing our offenses? *I think that is Santa.*

Is God putting stars or black check marks next to our names for each sin or indiscretion? *I think that is your teacher.* Does God remember every wrong move, poor choice, nasty comment or warped thought? *I think that is your spouse.*

God is not just a greyer, wiser, bigger one of us. God is God beyond all human understanding. For those on the spiritual

Fr. J Munley

journey, we slowly come to realize that God cannot be as small as we are, as petty as we are, or as unforgiving, because if that were so, we would not be able to rejoice in the gift of God's salvation. The abundance of God's love and mercy must far exceed our deepest longings.

QUESTIONS

What are some of the traits, characteristics, or understandings of God?

How does God reward or punish his people in your mind?

Is your God a vengeful God or one of mercy and compassion?

If we have free will, how does God intervene in our lives without jeopardizing that freedom?

Do you still hold to the understandings of God you were taught in first grade or have you grown in your relationship with God to a more mature understanding?

Does God have a face to you? What does that face look like? Why?

What is the difference between the 'Church' and 'God'? *(They are not one and the same)*. Have you been able to separate the two in order to see the difference between human shortcomings and divine will and action?

Personal notes:

God's breath

God's breath

SCRIPTURE "On the evening of that first day of the week, when the doors were locked, where the disciples were, for fear of the Jews, Jesus came and stood in their midst and said to them, "Peace be with you.". When he said this, he showed them his hands and his side. The disciples rejoiced when they saw the Lord. Jesus said to them again, "Peace be with you. As the Father has sent me, so I now I send you. And when he said this, he breathed on them and said to them, "Receive the Holy Spirit." **John 20: 19-22**

REFLECTION

Are we better off as a world, as a country, or as a church at this time in history or are we worse?

Is there any more compassion; any more love; any more life because we know Jesus Christ?

The first word Jesus speaks in the Gospel of John after his resurrection is one of "Peace". He then breathes the Holy Spirit not just onto the disciples but into the church. The feast of Pentecost is the celebration of the birth of the church.

The scriptures are filled with images of fire, life, love, peace, diversity with the call to unity which binds these gifts together. And yet it seems at times that we are far from being the people we are called to be.

What I have come to realize over the years is one simple truth: We are called to be of one Spirit, ***but not necessarily one mind.***

We may differ on ideas but still be of one spirit only if **charity** is present. Charity is the virtue that calls us as God's people to love beyond our own capacities. We are given a spirit of strength and conviction for both loving service and unselfish actions. If charity is lacking in our endeavors and relationships, we will have failed in our attempts at the Christian life. We cannot celebrate the feast of Pentecost without first acknowledging we have failed often to respect the differing ideas, lifestyles, cultures and beliefs of others.

Fr. J Munley

Through our honest assessment, we can then come to realize that we need our God more than ever. We need this peaceful spirit which Christ holds out to us. Not just today, but everyday.

The extreme factions of the 'right' and 'left' in media, government and religious institutions often times lack the one thing that would make it possible for them to be heard beyond their own narrow views; **Charity**. The extremists among us seem to care very little about the lives and views of anyone outside their own belief. True Christianity is left on the cutting room floor for more personal and selfish creeds.

In the Eucharist, we celebrate the birth of the church by the giving of the Holy Spirit by Christ Jesus. I believe the future of our church as **'one church' and 'One Body'**, rests in the ability to realize that we may not be of one mind, **but we must be united in spirit … God's spirit.** We must continue to call upon the Spirit of God for forgiving, loving and learning. The peace we seek, the love we are called to and the unity we desire, are not possible on our own. We have proven that again and again. We must each seek the life of Christ within our own lives, calling us to temper our tongues, widen our views and deepen our hearts.

QUESTIONS

Do you consider yourself a disciple of Christ? Why or Why not?

What is a disciple anyway, if we are all called to be one? What is your definition? Do you know how your church defines it?

How do you find, acknowledge and activate the Spirit of God within your own life?

Does prayer always have to be a ritual action? Can it be a moment or an experience?

Have you ever stopped to contemplate if the Spirit is alive in you, in your family, in your church? How? What makes it manifest and present?

If you cannot see or touch this Spirit, how do you know it is present or not?

Personal notes:

I don't understand

I don't understand

SCRIPTURE "When you see a cloud rising in the west you say immediately that is going to rain...and so it does; and when you notice that the wind is blowing from the south you say that it is going to be hot...and so it is. You hypocrites! You know how to interpret the appearance of the earth and the sky; why do you not know how to interpret the present time?" **Luke 12: 54-56**

REFLECTION

In his book, **New Seeds of Contemplation**, Thomas Merton wrote:

"When the whole world is in moral confusion, when no one knows any longer what to think, and when, in fact, everybody is running away from the responsibility of thinking, when man makes rational thought about moral issues absurd by exiling himself entirely from realities into the realm of fictions, and when he expends all his efforts into constructing more fictions with which to account for his ethical failures, then it becomes clear that the world cannot be saved from global war and global destruction by the mere efforts and good intentions of peacemakers."

If we have the humility to admit we can be or may be wrong, we can begin to see the **one truth** that will start to solve our ethical, cultural and political problems. We can all be more or less wrong, that we are all at fault; we are all limited and obstructed by our mixed motives, our self-deception, our greed and our self righteousness. This self truth could be the way toward a world community set on the goal of greater understanding and tolerance.

Blessed are the peacemakers and those who are strong enough and loud enough to challenge those wallowing in their own hatred and the wars they begin because they are afraid. Blessed are the meek and those who depend on others for sustenance. Blessed are those who work for the most vulnerable and despised of the world. Blessed be our God who calls each of us beyond our own limited world view to see the incredible gifts of many races, languages and ways of life.

QUESTIONS

From who or what do you receive the information that creates your world view and shapes your thoughts? Do you limit your intake to only those places or people who support what you already believe?

Do you blindly believe what you see and hear on television and radio? Why do we give so much power to biased media?

Do you think that those who disagree with your opinions may also have part of the truth? Or are you so sure of your positions that you never entertain the idea that you may be wrong? We all may be wrong? We all may have part of the truth?

Personal notes:

In between diapers

In between diapers

SCRIPTURE "Hear me, O coastlands, listen, O distant peoples. The Lord called me from birth, from my mother's womb he gave me my name. You are my servant, he said to me, through whom I show my glory. I will make you a light to the nations, that my salvation may reach to the ends of the earth. For thus says the Lord: in the time of favor I answer you, on the day of salvation I help you, To restore the land and allot the desolate heritages, Saying to the prisoners: Come out! To those in darkness; Show yourselves!" **Isaiah 49: 1-9**

REFLECTION

Isn't it funny? We come into the world and we are dressed with diapers and we leave this world dressed with diapers. Whether we are 2 or 92, it seems that most of us will find ourselves almost totally dependent on others. People start making our choices for us; telling us where to live and how to live; helping us eat and go to the bathroom.

I was never faced with the decision to put my parents in a nursing home. They both passed away too early, too young. The decision to place a parent in a nursing home has to be one of the most difficult decisions for the children of elderly parents. There are times when a nursing home is the only real option. But just the same, I am not a big fan. But, the fact is, we all want to live in our own homes until we die. Sometimes that is just not possible. I think it is at times heroic for children to take an ailing parent into their home. But how many times have parents taken their children back to live with them after thinking the children were finally out on their own.

My Grandmother lived in her own home up until her death at 92. She was half blind and getting more fragile by the day but by God she wanted to live in her own home until she croaked and she did. I was proud of her and her grit and determination.

We must value our elderly and the life they are '**still**' living; in nursing homes, in their children's homes or maybe, with a little luck and a prayer, even in their own homes. I just hope, when the time comes, I can wet myself with all the dignity I can muster in **my own home**.

Questions

Have you spent much time contemplating 'end of life' issues that may affect you? i.e.: Durable Power of Attorney, last wishes, final care arrangements, funeral options?

Why do you think most people do not want to discuss death?

Do you have a trusted friend you can discuss these issues with?

Do you think if you talk about death you are somehow hastening your own demise?

Have you thought about putting your wishes in writing for your family?

Personal notes:

I putze, therefore I am

Lunch break with God, Vol. 1

I putze, therefore I am

SCRIPTURE "Anyone who would not work should not eat. We hear that some of you are unruly, not keeping busy but acting like busybodies. We enjoin all such, and we urge them strongly in the Lord Jesus Christ, to earn the food they eat by working quietly. You must never grow weary of doing what is right, brothers and sisters."
2 Thes 3: 10-13

REFLECTION

Putzing must be genetically transmitted. My Dad was a putzer and I know I have inherited it from him.

I am a putzer, too. That is what I do, I putze. People who are puzters like to work with tools, and saws and backhoes and stuff like that. We like to wax the car, shine the rims, clean the windows, and some times we'll even vacuum the floor. The difference between those who putze and everyone else is that... *we like it*. We like to wash the car. We like to clean the garage. We find joy in a job well done. We pick up, clean up, sweep up.

Work. Simple, uncomplicated work. It clears the mind. It puts us back in rhythm with life. I know why some farmers would never think of doing anything else. They toil and labor all day in the fields, in the earth and see their work combine with nature to provide crops for our food. There is something very satisfying about good, hard work; the kind of work that wears you to the bone.

There is a big difference between being physically tired and emotionally worn out. So much of our lives now are filled with information overload. We are bombarded with mind boggling tragedy and heartache at every turn. It is good to take time to reconnect with the most basic things in life by getting our hands dirty.

QUESTIONS

What do you do to relieve stress? Do you have a hobby or personal interest that allows you to unwind and relax?

What connects you to the earth or the seasons of nature?

If you use your hands for a living, can you find an interest to use your mind? If you work from a desk, what do you do to engage your hands?

Personal notes:

Love, quiet, shhh, peace

Lunch break with God, Vol. 1

Love, quiet, shhh, peace

SCRIPTURE Leaving the crowd, they took him with them in the boat just as he was. And other boats were with him. A violent squall came up and waves were breaking over the boat, so that it was already filling up. Jesus was in the stern, asleep on a cushion. They woke him and said to him, "Teacher, do you not care that we are perishing?" He woke up, rebuked the wind, and said to the sea, "Quiet! Be still!" The wind ceased and there was great calm."

Mk 4:36–39

REFLECTION

Love: Is it possible without someone asking for repayment?
Expecting reimbursement?
Holding others captive?
Does love ever just come without strings?
Unconditional?

Quiet: Try being quiet. It is a rare art form.
Not a science.
Can you turn off the brain?
Can you stop that churning, thinking, non-stop machine?
Yes, it is a rare art.

Shhh! Try not talking for awhile
Don't say anything.
Silence is the heart of all contemplation....

Peace. It is a lifetime,
Of searching, striving, failing
Peace comes only after war.

QUESTIONS

Why is it so difficult for some of us to turn off our brains? Why must we constantly do "mental gymnastics"?

What kind of concentration, charisma, self-understanding, or effort does it take to develop a calm mind?

Is it possible that what we so actively seek is actually about exerting no effort at all? Is it possible a quiet mind comes from a quiet interior life? How does that come about?

Personal notes:

My father was a gentleman

My father was a gentleman

SCRIPTURE "My son, if your heart be wise, my own heart also will rejoice; And my inmost being will exult, when your lips speak what is right. Let not your heart emulate sinners, but be zealous for the fear of the Lord always; For you will surely have a future, and your hope will not be cut off … Listen to your father who begot you, and despise not your mother when she is old … The father of a just man will exult with glee; he who begets a wise son will have joy in him."
Prv 23:15–18, 22, 24

REFLECTION

My Father was a gentleman. It was part of who he was. He held himself with dignity and grace. He liked some things the way they were—romantic music, good scotch, a hot barbecue—and family everywhere. The more the merrier.

His hair was pure white—my father. He always said it was because of us (his kids). I knew he was right. I also knew I added to that grey.

I loved to watch my parents dance. They moved together with poise and grace. I think one of the greatest gifts my dad gave to his children is that he loved our mother. He loved my mom through thick and thin, good and bad; in health and through sickness.

My father was a man of his word. When he said he would do something, be somewhere, help someone, he meant it and he did it. He loved to tell a joke and would laugh harder than anyone.

My dad had a way of making our darkest moments bright. His famous saying was, "It's not the end of the world, it's just the end of the day." We were always afraid to tell him we flunked the class, wore his socks, or wrecked the car. But it was always the same. After a few swear words, a couple of "What's wrong with you kids?" and maybe a kick in the pants, it was time to deal with the problem and make it right.

"Grandpa" was a name my father cherished. I think some of his happiest moments occurred when one grandchild was on his lap and one had a stranglehold on his neck. With grandkids, he was able to offer his sage wisdom to a whole new generation.

My father was a true "church man." He supported the church financially, prayerfully, and wholeheartedly. My dad was not a perfect human being, just a darn good one. Integrity, honesty, and family marked his life. He has left the world a little better because he was in it. He has left a legacy.

One day, when I grow up, I want to be just like him.

QUESTIONS

What words spring to mind when you think about your father/dad?

Can you rejoice in what your father was/is?

Can you forgive your father for what he was/is not?

Can you create the family you always thought would be the kind of loving and caring family you imagined?

ACTION PLAN

Take an honest assessment of your relationship with your father. Write down two things that you are thankful for and two areas in which you need healing.

Personal notes:

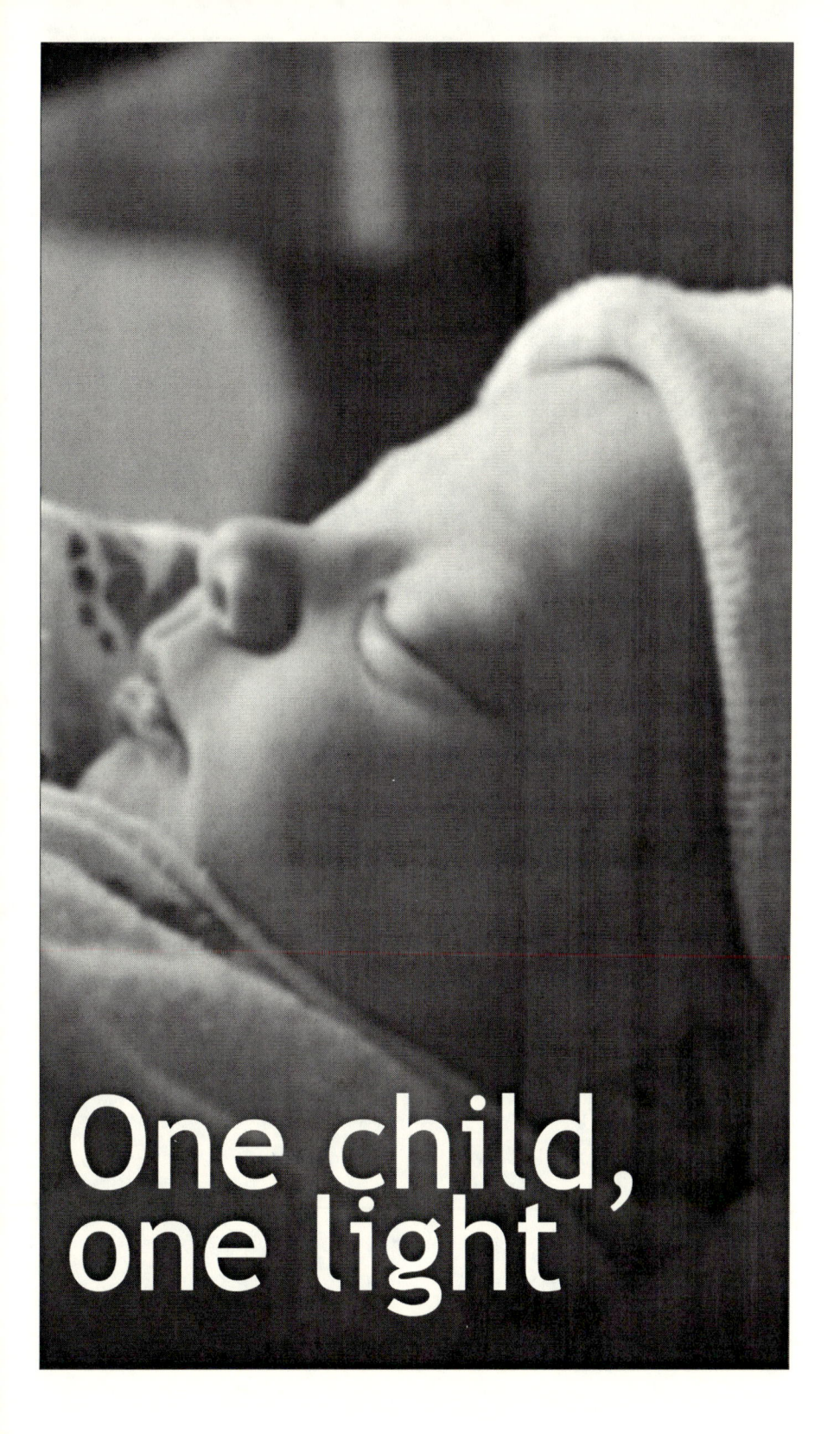

One child, one light

One child, one light

SCRIPTURE Asked by the Pharisees when the kingdom of God would come, Jesus said in reply, "The coming of the kingdom of God cannot be observed, and no one will announce, 'Look, here it is,' or, 'There it is.' For behold, the kingdom of God is among you."
Lk 17:20-21

REFLECTION

> The Kingdom is here
> In fits and starts
> In yeast and new wine
> In bread for the hungry
> Water for the thirsty
> For one and all
>
> The Kingdom is here
> But not yet
> Not quite
> Not fully
>
> The Kingdom is here
> And the light has come
> The darkness cannot overcome the light
> For it shines on in the dark
>
> And He is born again
> On this day, in this place
> In you and me

QUESTIONS

Where have you found the kingdom of god alive in your life? What does it look like?

Who are the people who seem to help bring about the kingdom for others? Are you one of them?

If the kingdom is here and among us, why is the world in such a mess?

Fr. J Munley

ACTION PLAN

Do one simple thing tomorrow to make the world a little better place for someone else (put a flower on a coworker's desk, take someone who seems lonely to lunch, mow an elderly person's lawn or pay a stranger a compliment).

Personal notes:

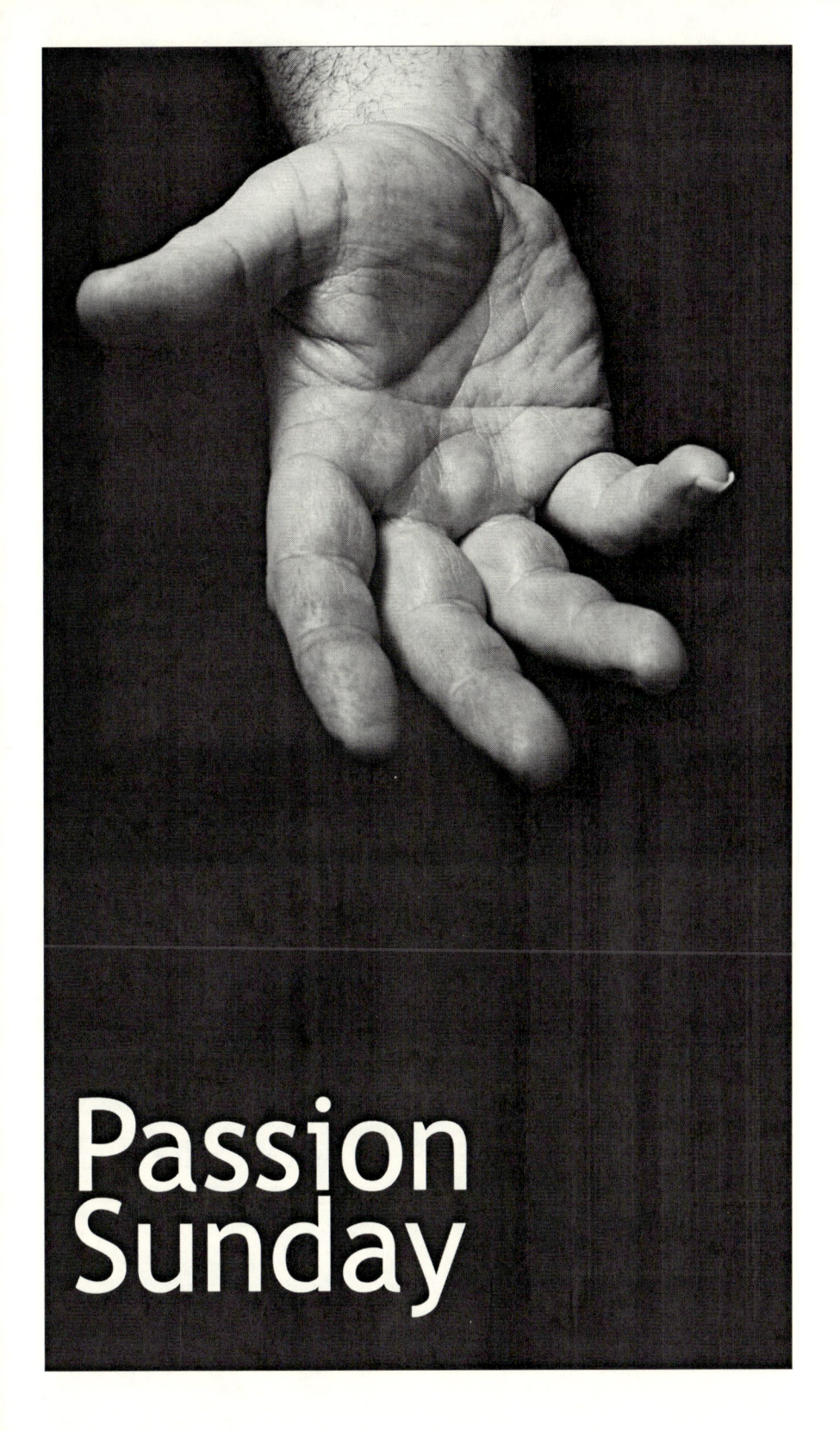

Passion Sunday

Passion Sunday

SCRIPTURE Then going out he went, as was his custom, to the Mount of Olives, and the disciples followed him. When he arrived at the place he said to them, "Pray that you may not undergo the test." After withdrawing about a stone's throw from them and kneeling, he prayed, saying, "Father, if you are willing, take this cup away from me; still, not my will but yours be done." [And to strengthen him an angel from heaven appeared to him. He was in such agony and he prayed so fervently that his sweat became like drops of blood falling on the ground.] When he rose from prayer and returned to his disciples, he found them sleeping from grief. He said to them, "Why are you sleeping? Get up and pray that you may not undergo the test."
Lk 22:39–46

REFLECTION

> How can the majority of people stay silent in a world complacent about war, unconscious of sexism, blasé about hunger, unmoved by the struggles of the elderly, and disdainful of poverty?
>
> Helen Keller may have identified the greatest affliction of them all: the lack of enthusiasm for life—for our own lives and the lives of others.
>
> The Passion of Jesus Christ we proclaim, celebrate, and announce is not the lustful, selfish, fleeting passion that we have come to know through daytime soap operas and blockbuster movies. It is first and foremost the passion of our God who came to wear our skin, sweat our sweat, and bleed our blood. It is a God who so intimately loved us that he became one of us in Jesus. This passion is the stuff of life in its greatest depth and width and breadth. It is also the hope of new life. Passion lights a fire where once only cold embers sat.
>
> The passion we proclaim through the Gospel is a profound and heartfelt commitment to life. It is a depth of participation in the human condition that evokes incredible compassion and calls us

beyond our self-interest to participation in the events of life that challenges the norm, uncover the weak human attempts for personal glory, confront the unquenchable thirst for power; this passion should bring us to our knees in humility.

This Gospel is the call to a passion for life. A life lived deeply and well. When we are weary and worn, we can renew our lives and our faith through this Jesus whose passion shunned personal glorification in favor of total self-giving. When confronted with evil, Jesus willingly and steadfastly entered into a prayerful and determined mission.

There are times we may find ourselves living in fear. Afraid to speak our beliefs; afraid to challenge the status quo; afraid to call industry, government, and religious institutions to accountability; and afraid to change in order to set ourselves free from that which holds us bound.

Passion; the God of passion made flesh in Jesus. This passion of which we speak is more than enthusiasm. It is seeing life for what it is and what it is not. We must decide if we have a voice and a spirit which we will use for the betterment of our families, our communities, and our world. Without this passion, this desire for life, we prematurely begin our own journey toward death.

Questions

Do you have a "passion" for life? If life has somehow dulled your senses, what would help to bring back that gift?

What is the difference between passion and lust or desire?

What fears may keep you from living life more fully or deeply? What is one way to eradicate fear?

PERSONAL NOTES:

Remember

Remember

SCRIPTURE "Finally, brothers, whatever is true, whatever is honorable, whatever is just, whatever is pure, whatever is lovely, whatever is gracious, if there is any excellence and if there is anything worthy of praise, think about these things. Keep on doing what you have learned and received and heard and seen in me. Then the God of peace will be with you ... I know indeed how to live in humble circumstances; I know indeed how to live in humble circumstances; I know also how to live with abundance. In every circumstance and in all things I have learned the secret of being well fed and of going hungry, of living in abundance and of being in need. I have the strength for everything through him who empowers me."
Phil 4:8–9, 12-13

REFLECTION

> I remember to this day the moment I learned how to do "longhand division." I can recall how I struggled to understand what the teacher actually wanted us to discover. How many times must she have demonstrated the problems on the blackboard? Suddenly, a light went off in my head and I understood. It was a breakthrough moment that has always stuck with me—such a minor event that held profound meaning. From that point on, math began to open up to me as a language all its own. It was the repetition that helped me to understand this secret language, and I felt like I was in on the secret. It is a great tragedy when we stop learning and discovering the many wonderful gifts life holds.
>
> We have very short memories. We need to be reminded again and again. We need to learn and re-learn what we once knew but may have forgotten. For hundreds of years, before the Scriptures where written down, they were told as stories—again and again until the children of the villages knew them by heart. Before the Scriptures were written, they were spoken to keep them alive, to keep the lessons before the people's eyes. We forget.

Fr. J Munley

Hence, we gather the people around both the "Table" and the "Word of God" every Sunday. We need to hear the words and actions of Jesus and listen to how his life changed human history and so many other countless lives in the process. Jesus certainly knew what he was doing when he told the disciples at the Last Supper: "Do this in memory of me."

It is difficult to learn the same lessons over and over again but it is also part of the human experience. We must learn and re-learn until at last we remember the lessons and we begin to live them. It is one thing to know and another to put what we know into practice. It is always in the living that the secrets of life take on meaning and truth.

What are the secrets of life? They are the things that have always been. They are the intangibles in life. The things we cannot see, hear, or touch but know they are present just the same. The secrets of life are the real gifts waiting to be discovered by each of us.

QUESTIONS

Can you remember a time when something you were struggling to understand finally became clear and you had an "ah hah" moment? What did it feel like? When was the last time you felt that kind of simple joy in learning?

What in life may be a "secret" that is really evident in the human experience but perhaps buried in our rushed and busy lives?

Have you thought about going back to school or finding new ways to learn something that is of interest to you? What is holding you back? There are always excuses; what are yours?

When was the last time you discovered something new about God? What was it and did it make you want to know more?

Great spiritual thinkers have called God 'The Known" and "The Unknown." Why do you suppose that is?

Personal notes:

Rose bud

Rose bud

SCRIPTURE When one finds a worthy wife, her value is far beyond pearls. Her husband entrusts his heart to her, has unfailing prize. She brings good and not evil, all the days of her life ... She rises while still night, and distributes food to her household ... She reaches out her hands to the poor, and extends her arms to the needy ... She is clothed with strength and dignity, and she laughs at the days to come ... Her children rise up and praise her; her husband, too extols her: "Many are the women of proven worth, but you have excelled them all."
Prv 31:10–12, 15, 20, 25, 28-29

REFLECTION

> You loved me before you knew me
> You were the first to call me by name
> That sweet sound would be the voice I would search for
> Even when my eyes could not yet see
> I knew I was safe
> One of the first words I would utter would be 'Mom"
> And I probably never stopped talking after that
>
> I think you were as scared as I was
> To go to school that first time, that first day
> You coxed me to the bus with hugs and kisses
> And then had to let me go
> It would be one of the many "leavings" we would experience together
>
> It was your arms that opened to hold me when I fell
> How many times would you have to pick me up?
> How many times would you have tell me it would be alright
> Who knew that a band-aid and a cookie could heal us so quickly?
>
> You never thought you were a good cook
> But still to this day, nothing compares
> You never thought you were pretty
> We thought you were the most beautiful thing on earth.
>
> You made our birthday's special events.

Fr. J Munley

They were not just another day
But a celebration day
I will always be grateful for that

Christmas was not a day to you
It was an event
It was filled with faith, fun and excitement
You would put each decoration out as if a priceless treasure
And now the memories themselves have become "priceless treasures"

You wanted your kids to be happy
You cried with us, laughed with us, and knew our sorrows
You taught us not to lie, but we did anyway
You taught us not to swear, but Dad taught us how to
And we knew we could always come home if we had to
Know matter how old we got

Your faith was simple, yet profound
Go to church on Sunday
Pray at every meal
Pick a favorite saint
And know that God loves you

Now that you are no longer with us
We realize more than ever
That what you said and what you did
Helped make us who we are

You watched over us here on earth
Now you watch over us from heaven
But a mother is a mother
From our first day to our last
Thank you for being ours.

QUESTIONS

How has your mother influenced your life for good or ill? Can you muster the maturity and depth of understanding to incorporate your mother's gifts while forgiving and releasing her for her shortcomings?

Are you the mother you hoped you would be? Or, as a man, are there virtues you can see in your mother or other women that would make you a better human being?

How would the world, the nation, or the church be different with more women in leadership roles? Would there be any difference at all? Can you temper your bias to see the possibilities?

Personal notes:

The gifted curse

The gifted curse

SCRIPTURE [Jesus told this parable.] "A sower went out to sow his seed. And as he sowed, some seed fell on the path and was trampled, and the birds of the sky ate it up. Some seed fell on rocky ground, and when it grew, it withered for lack of moisture. Some seed fell among thorns, and the thorns grew with it and choked it. And some seed fell on good soil, and when it grew, it produced fruit a hundredfold." After saying this, he called out, "Whoever has ears to hear ought to hear."
Lk 8:5–8

REFLECTION

Every one of us should be able to name and claim some of the gifts we possess as individuals. But I know that this is not always the case. When asked to name a personal gift we possess, we will stumble and stutter and wonder what in fact those gifts might be. They do not come readily to mind. It is important to study our own giftedness, for within each gift is also a curse. In every personality and individual lies the seed of something great and wonderful. Tagging closely behind is the opposite of that gift which lays dormant until one or the other is called out of sleep. To know both "the gift and curse" is indeed the seed of personal enlightenment.

One of my gifts is turning a "sow's ear" into a "silk purse." I like to take old things and make them look new. I like to sand and rub and polish until what once was may become visible again. I enjoy seeing new possibilities and solutions in old problems. My mind is always at work on some invention or concoction.

The curse of a "recovering perfectionist" is that it is hard to leave well enough alone. I see every bent angle, crooked line, and off-center placement. My mind's eye is like a magnet to those things that are askew. However, I am also learning that sometimes, good enough has to be good enough.

My gift and curse demonstrate that a double-edged sword often accompanies such traits. A perfectionist strives for great precision and symmetry. We like things a certain way and will work to make it so. But not all things carry the same importance or significance. We have to know when to put a thing down. When to stop and when to let go and realize we have given it all it needs for now. It is a continual lesson in "letting go." I wonder if age and wisdom are the only way into this balancing act. Perhaps what we thought to be a curse is actually a gift!

QUESTIONS

What aspects of your life are just good enough so you can give time and energy to something else? Name one thing that would fall into this category.

What are some of your gifts? What is the double-edged sword that comes with your gift; your curse? Are there any negatives associated with your gifts?

Do you feel that naming your gifts is like bragging? What does humility have to do with this?

Personal notes:

The many paths to peace

The many paths to peace

SCRIPTURE "I, then, a prisoner for the Lord, urge you to live in a manner worthy of the call you have received, with all humility and gentleness, with patience, bearing with one another through love, striving to preserve the unity of the spirit through the bond of peace: one body and one Spirit, as you were also called to the one hope of your call; one Lord, one faith, one baptism; one God and Father of all, who is over all and through all and in all."
Eph 4:1–6

REFLECTION

Recently the test to become a U.S. Citizen was revamped and the questions made more relevant and thought provoking. One of the questions on the new test is: "Name one meaningful statement of belief in the Declaration of Independence."

One of the answers is: "All men and women are created equal."

Sometimes the answers we seek to peace are hiding in plain sight, right in our face, right in the very fiber and framework of our own country's beliefs—we all are created equal. Not that we have the same gifts or talents or intellect. But we are equal in our humanness; we are equal in the sight of God and others.

The question really becomes, "Do we believe it? Do we believe we are created equal?" Our history would suggest many have not believed it. This is about the very nature of being human. It is the recognition that we all have not just the need but the right to be respected and nurtured; that there is freedom and justice for all.

It is about realizing that the gift of life is to be held as the greatest gift above all other things. All life is worthy and precious. Mutual respect is the only path to lasting peace. We have a long way to go, don't we?

QUESTIONS

Have we learned any lessons from the fragile history of our country and the world on the way of human relations?

What is one thing that you have learned in meeting people of other faiths, races or ways of life?

Are you able to respect those with whom you have fundamental differences or do you always see them as an enemy?

How do we overcome our own prejudices and blindness?

How does faith and prayer heighten our awareness of the dignity all people deserve?

Personal notes:

The secret

The secret

SCRIPTURE "Come to me, all you who labor and are burdened, and I will give you rest. Take my yoke upon you and learn from me, for I am meek and humble of heart; and you will find rest for yourselves. For my yoke is easy and my burden light."
Mt 11:28–30

REFLECTION

> What is this secret, hidden from the learned and clever,
> What is it; that escapes the wise.
> Where is this jewel that Jesus spoke to us about
> The Kingdom that evil will despise
>
> If our faith is so simple
> Why do our leaders make it so hard?
> Whose yoke are we towing
> Whose faith do we regard?
>
> If Jesus called it easy
> And a burden that was light
> Why do I feel so heavy?
> Why does it feel like a fight?
>
> When will we capture the essence?
> Of who Christ came to be
> When will our faith be life giving
> When will I know I am free?
>
> Lord, you called us to table
> You ask us to do what you did
> So give us the eyes of the Spirit
> Help us to see what you hid
>
> The Kingdom is finally here now
> And yet it is far away
> When will we stop the violence?
> When will we see that day?
> Where hatred is quenched by mercy

Fr. J Munley

When love is here to stay

Loosen our stubborn hearts, Lord
Teach us how to pray
That all you taught, and lived, and gave
May all be ours some day.

Personal notes:

Today is the day the Lord has made

Today is the day the Lord has made

SCRIPTURE "When they had gathered together they asked him, "Lord, are you at this time going to restore the kingdom to Israel?" He answered them, "It is not for you to know the times or seasons that the Father has established by his own authority. But you will receive power when the holy Sprit comes upon you, and you will be my witnesses in Jerusalem, throughout Judea and Samaria, and to the ends of the earth." When he had said this, as they were looking on, he was lifted up, and a cloud took him from their sight. **Acts 1:6–9**

REFLECTION

I want to tell you a story.

It is a story of life and death. It is a story of faith and hope.

It is a true story.

After she was diagnosed with cancer, for two years she fought but in the last few months of her life, it was becoming apparent she was losing the battle. The call came on Holy Thursday; this was it. Probably today, the family was told. Everyone gathered around her as they had so many times in the last few days. Everyone wanted to be there. The day lingered and so did she. It was painful for the family to watch. Slowly, quietly, long breaths, but she held on.

And so came Good Friday. The family thought, "This would be a good day." Christ's passion and death. To be joined to that day and to Jesus in his suffering. Again, it was not meant to be.

Holy Saturday came and the family gathered in the living room around their dying mother, getting ready to return to their homes again for the journey they had made so many times. The priest said that he would return tomorrow, Easter Sunday, to have Mass with the family at 1:30 in the afternoon.

That Sunday, that Easter Sunday, as all the family began to arrive, the dying woman began to fade. Her breath was shallow. It was approaching the end. One daughter was yet to arrive.

She came into the house a few minutes before 1:30, thinking the Mass would be about to begin. As 1:30 came, right at the time the family was to celebrate the Easter Mass; the woman breathed her last, and was gone.

After the crying, the hugging, and the shock of what had just happened sunk in to all who gathered, the family moved around the dining room table, and celebrated Mass. The Mass of the resurrection. The Mass of new life.

That family is my family. The dying mother was my mother.

The pain of her loss still stings, but what she left us remains. She left the gift of knowing that we were loved, not perfectly, but well. She left a legacy of the importance of family and the joy of our gathering that still lasts to this day. She left us the gift of humor and laughter. I see her best qualities in my sisters and smile when they don't know I am watching them because I see our mother in them.

My mother left us the gift of faith. Her faith was simple yet profound. It was what sustained her and ultimately what sustained us to walk with her in her dying.

So many people want a sign that their loved one is with God. A rose, a bird on the windowsill, the smell of their perfume, or their favorite song. My mother's sign, I believe, was that she left us just as we were to ask God to be with us in the Mass of resurrection. She went to God and God came to us, at the dining room table.

This brings us to the feast of the Ascension. Jesus left his family and those he loved, and asked them to carry on. He left them his stories and his life. He left them his spirit and the gift of love to be shared with others. He left them the legacy of the Christian family. He disappeared from their view, but lives on in the lives of those who tell his story, who seek his spirit and who imitate his virtue and compassion.

My mother did not leave us, but lives on in us, her family.

As the disciples were losing their faith after the death of Jesus, he appeared to them with the message that he would be with them always, until the end of the world. This is where we find our hope. This is where we find our life. When we know that the life and story of Jesus is our life and story, we find our reason to rejoice in his message that life has changed, not ended.

Jesus did not leave us, but lives on in us, his family.

QUESTIONS

Every family has a gift to offer, even the most dysfunctional. What gifts can you focus on from your family that has helped to make you who you are?

Can you forgive the shortcomings of your family of origin in order to focus on the gift of life now? How much time do you spend focusing on the past and what you feel you did not receive from your family? At what point do you need to forgive and move on? What will that take?

What do you need to do now in order to save yourself from regret when your parents, spouse, or loved ones pass away?

PERSONAL NOTES:

What are we praying for?

What are we praying for?

SCRIPTURE "And I tell you, ask and you will receive; seek and you will find; knock and the door will be opened to you. For everyone who asks, receives; and the one who seeks, finds; and to the one who knocks, the door will be opened. What father among you would hand his son a snake when he asks for a fish? Or hand him a scorpion when he asks for an egg? If you then, who are wicked, know how to give good gifts to your children, how much more will the Father in heaven give the holy Spirit to those who ask him?"
Lk 11:9–13

REFLECTION

>Patrick was driving down the street in a sweat because he had an important meeting and couldn't find a parking place. Looking up to heaven, he prayed, "Lord take pity on me. If you find me a parking place I will go to Mass every Sunday for the rest of my life and give up my Irish whiskey." Miraculously, a parking place appeared.
>
>Patrick looked up to heaven again and said, "Never mind, I found one."
>
>What are we praying for? Literally, why do we pray and what are we asking of God? The reasons for prayer are many and varied. We pray to give glory to God, to praise the maker of the universe and the one who set the sun in the sky. We pray in thanksgiving, for the gift of life and people who become our family. We sing praise to God, because when we sing, we pray twice and music is the language of angels. We pray in petition to God, asking God to favor us and grant our prayer. We pray in stunned silence when we are faced with the grandeur of God, and we are forced to our knees in humility.
>
>But we also pray because we are needy. We came into this world dependent on God and others and we will leave this world in the same way. But on our journey of life, we find ourselves asking God many questions: What is the meaning of life? Why are people the way they are? Why are we living the lives we are

living? We ask and sometimes the answer comes right away. But mostly our answers from God come over time. Not because God is slow to respond, but because we are slow to understand.

In a world of microwave dinners, fast food from a drive-in window, the world at our fingertips by computer...we expect things fast and want our answers faster. But for God who is infinite and does not move to a ticking clock, our timetable may not be his. We see the world from our limited and often small perspective. If we are to seek answers from God, we must also be willing to persist in the questions. Persistence may actually be the hallmark of a strong prayer life.

Sometimes it is easier to say what prayer is not.
• Prayer is not magic a la Harry Potter
• Prayer is not a vending machine—in goes a quarter's worth of prayer, out comes the gumball of my desire
• Prayer is not the lottery—two Our Fathers and the Powerball number makes you rich

No, prayer is more like a mirror. It is meant to reflect back to us the God life within. Prayer is meant to hold the truth up close so we can see ourselves for who we are in the sight of God and others. Prayer speaks a word of hope in the dark.

We are told by Jesus to seek, knock, and ask and it will be ours. The secret to this riddle is that we must read the entire passage. Jesus explains that spiritual gifts will be ours in abundance. If we are seeking the spiritual gifts, then our God holds them out to us freely and without reservations. If we are seeking the things of this world, we need to buy a lottery ticket.

QUESTIONS

Do you contemplate the meaning of life and what are some of your conclusions?

What is the ultimate meaning of life?

What gives your life meaning?

How do you pray? Do you have a tendency to ask God for material things? What is at the heart of your normal prayer?

Do you ever pray in gratitude, wonder, for healing or insight? Why or why not?

PERSONAL NOTES:

What if?

Lunch break with God, Vol. 1

What if?

SCRIPTURE ... Jesus, tired from his journey, sat down there at the well. It was about noon. A woman of Samaria came to draw water. Jesus said to her, "Give me a drink." His disciples had gone into the town to buy food. The Samaritan woman said to him, "How can you, a Jew, ask me a Samaritan woman, for a drink?" Jesus answered and said to her, "If you knew the gift of God and who is saying to you, 'Give me a drink,' you would have asked him and he would have given you living water." ... Sir you do not even have a bucket and the cistern is deep; where than can you get this living water? Are you greater than our father Jacob, who gave us this cistern and drank from it himself with his flocks? Jesus answered and said to her, "Everyone who drinks this water will be thirsty again; but whoever drinks the water I shall give will never thirst; the water I shall give will become in him a spring of water welling up to eternal life." The woman said to him, "Sir give me this water, so That I may not be thirsty or have to keep coming here to draw water." Jesus said to her, "Go call your husband and come back." The woman answered and said to him, "I do not have a husband," Jesus answered her, "You are right in saying, 'I do not have a husband.' For you have had five husband and the one you have now is not your husband ... "Sir, I can see that you are a prophet." ... The woman said to him, "I know that the Messiah is coming, the one called the Anointed; when he comes, he will tell us everything." Jesus said to her, "I am he, the one who is speaking with you." ... The woman left her water jar and went into the town and said to the people, "Come see a man who told me everything I have done. Could he be the Messiah?"
Jn 4:6-19, 25, 28-29

REFLECTION

> What if God were an old woman who wore red hats and white linen dresses with shoes that didn't match and she had pure white hair that fell to her knees.
> What if God were an old woman, so old that time did not know her and the earth was but a child in her yawning and the sun rose from the palm of her hand.

What if God wore her wrinkles like badges of courage and her hands were worn from holding the broken-hearted, the addicted, the fallen, the outcast and the lonely.
What if God were colorblind and saw the beauty of her creatures only from the inside out. What if God decided that sin was sad, but that love was stronger.

What if God were an old woman who rocked on the porch and smoked big cigars and didn't worry about being politically correct as a way to mask the truth and hide behind nice language all the while dancing with one's own defenses.

What if God thought sexuality was a gift to be used to unify and not a moral stamp to label "who's in and who's out."

What if God were an old woman who winked and smiled a lot, all the while touching each person on the hand with a gentle pat saying, "That's alright honey, you're forgiven." What if it were as easy as that. What if the hoops, and jumps, and flips we do in the name of religion weren't part of the original plan, but were added later without approval.

What if God were an old woman, whose eyes were ageless and danced in shimmers of light that saw through our protests and pulled back the curtain of our own lies, the ones we tell ourselves only in passing shadows of mirrored truth, to reveal the reality of who we really are, only to find she loves us anyway.

What if God were an old woman who thought we had too many rules, too many preconceived ideas of who she was – too many religions – too many roadblocks to her house. What if she just wanted us to come to her house on Sunday, drink a few beers, eat some chicken and talk about our lives. What if she just wanted to love us and in turn for us to love her and then each other.

What if God were an old woman who disguised herself as a young man, and sat by a well, waiting, just waiting, for us to stumble by.

Questions

What is your idea, your image of God? Is it always a man, always stern, always keeping track of your sins and errors?

What does your idea and understanding reveal about you? What does it say about the way you were raised? Has your view of God ever changed through prayer, meditation, life experiences, or encounters?

What would help expand your knowledge, love, or idea of God? Have you ever thought about praying a totally different way than you presently do to feed your spirit? Would you consider yoga, meditation, spiritual reading if you do not have any of these forms of prayer in your life?

What value do you see to variations in your prayer life?

Personal notes:

When Easter comes

When Easter comes

SCRIPTURE After the Sabbath, as the first day of the week was dawning, Mary Magdalene and the other Mary came to see the tomb. And behold, there was a great earthquake; for an angel of the Lord descended from heaven, approached, rolled back the stone, and sat upon it. His appearance was like lightning and his clothing was white as snow. The guards were shaken with fear of him and became like dead men. Then the angel said to the women in reply, "Do not be afraid! I know that you are seeking Jesus the crucified. He is not here, for he has been raised just as he said. Come and see the place where he lay. Then go quickly and tell his disciples, 'He has been raised from the dead, and he is going before you to Galilee; there you will see him.' Behold, I have told you." Then they went away quickly from the tomb, fearful yet overjoyed, and ran to announce this to his disciples. And behold, Jesus met them on their way and greeted them. They approached, embraced his feet, and did him homage. Then Jesus said to them, "Do not be afraid. Go tell my brothers to go to Galilee, and there they will see me."
Mt 28:1-10

REFLECTION

Resurrection didn't happen this year. At least not for me and not according to the date we are supposed to gather and celebrate new life in Christ Jesus. The truth is that resurrection doesn't happen according to a calendar. Resurrection happens when and where we need it. We cannot schedule resurrection.

Resurrection is not just for those who have left this world in death – resurrection has something to say to the living. There is something that must happen for us here and now: Can the resurrection speak a word of hope to us? Does this gift of new life have something to offer to those weighed down by fear, pulled down by life, brought low by divorce, grief, abuse, or health?

Our lives are actually a series of small deaths and resurrections. Sometimes the resurrection we need just doesn't happen when and how we think it should or want it to. Sometimes we are not ready for resurrection; we are not done dying. We aren't done grieving or suffering or getting over the shock of sorrow. We need to wallow and stir in our misery for a while. Some people never leave that prison ... that place of death, without new life.

But what about those who want it? What does it take to embrace it, this new life, this resurrection? We need to be ready. Maybe we need to pray first for the desire for new life. And then the hope of God raising our souls from the dust becomes the first light in the darkness.

We will spend our lifetime dying and rising. It is that movement of life to death that focuses our sights on what is important: always changing, always growing, and always letting go. If we are to learn anything from the disciples in the gospel, I think it is that we cannot grasp what is not ours to hold. We can only learn to live in joyful hope and the peace Jesus came to pour out on this people.

We cannot force, grasp, or hold on to resurrection. It is an unfolding over time. We must let it "happen" within us. Resurrection is the hope of spring in the winter of the soul. It is the seed that breaks ground and flowers. It is the very life of Jesus, calling us from the darkness to light.

QUESTIONS

What mini-deaths have you experienced that need resurrection: divorce, depression, illness, sorrow or grief?

What will aid you in finding life in the midst of these deaths?

What do you think resurrection will be like? Heaven? God? (Spend some time thinking about these realities.)

What gives people without faith ... hope? Have you ever found yourself despairing and without hope? Who or what brings that gift to you?

Personal notes:

Would we kill him again?

Lunch break with God, Vol. 1

Would we kill him again?

SCRIPTURE "Hear another parable. There was a landowner who planted a vineyard, put a hedge around it, dug a wine press in it, and built a tower. Then he leased it to tenants and went on a journey. When vintage time drew near, he sent his servants to the tenants to obtain his produce. But the tenants seized the servants and one they beat, another they killed, and a third they stone. Again he sent other servants, more numerous than the first ones, but they treated them in the same way. Finally, he sent his son to them, thinking, 'They will respect my son.' But when the tenants saw the son, they said to one another, 'This is the heir. Come, let us kill him and acquire his inheritance.' They seized him, threw him out of the vineyard, and killed him. What will the owner of the vineyard do to those tenants when he comes?" They answered him, "He will put those wretched men to a wretched death and lease his vineyard to other tenants who will give him the produce at the proper time."
MT 21:33-41

REFLECTION

> If he came into our town, our home, our lives, and asked us not to worry, to love beyond measure, told us that suffering was coming, would we listen? Would we open our hearts? Would we change our lives?
>
> What if he said our country was too rich? What if he said we were too stubborn and too arrogant? What if he thought we were too violent and sometimes downright mean? What if he thought we had lost all respect for life? Not just new life but old life as well. What if he challenged us to see our lives as more than just our own, to see our elderly as more than just a drain, to see children for who they are and not for who we want them to be?
>
> Would we listen, let down our guard, change?
>
> What is this Jesus came here ... now and told us the kingdom of God was already in our midst? Where is it? What if he said it begins from within and then gets lived from without? What if that was the secret? What if we thought him insane? The truth

we waited to hear, but could not bring ourselves to believe; because it seemed so far beyond us. Would we need to silence him? Would we need to quiet this man who gave us what we needed but could not fulfill all we wanted, because we are insatiable, always wanting something more, chasing something more, hoping for something more.

Does he bring the good news, or is this news just another problem, a stumbling block to doing what we want to do? What if he said the poor were rich, the humble and meek were powerful, the sorrowful would laugh, and children held the key to his kingdom? Would we think him mad?

What if he told us to melt our missiles into plowshares and our guns into harvest tools?
What if he knew the way to peace, but it meant giving up vengeance, retaliation, and war? Could we do it? Would we do it?
Will this Jesus live in us, through us, and with us?
Will the kingdom of heaven be ours, or will it be given to another?

Questions

As stewards of Earth and the kingdom, how do you feel we are doing with what has been entrusted to us? How are you doing with your stewardship and what you have been entrusted with?

Personal notes:

_____

_____

_____

_____

_____

_____

_____